"*50 Things You Can Do About Guns* is a practical guide for those who want to know what they can do about violence in their neighborhoods. Sometimes the most basic solutions evade us when we are confronted with complex social problems, such as the proliferation of handguns in America. This book provides common sense solutions. It is not just another book on guns; it is a tool that each of us can use, in a constructive non-violent way, to stop the madness in our streets."

> – **Joe Sciacca**
> **Political Editor**
> *Boston Herald*

"If you're fed up with hearing about another shooting on the local news, a new guide can help you stop the violence. *50 Things You Can Do About Guns*, by Boston anti-gun activist James M. Murray, provides tips on organizing a gun 'buy-back' program in your community, practicing 'toy gun control' in your home, catching deadly loopholes in your local gun laws, and dozens of other actions. This practical book is also loaded with alarming figures on the extent of the gun problem.... [Murray] suggests that *anyone* can do something about the epidemic of shootings: 'Don't be put off or intimidated because you may not be an *expert* on guns and gun laws. The fact that you live in this country qualifies you as an expert on gun violence'."

> – **Dan Fields**
> **Editor**
> **"The New Age Networker"**
> *New Age Journal*
> May/June 1994

"Everyone's talking about guns these days, but very few people know what to do about them. James M. Murray, organizer of the community group CeaseFire, Boston, offers not only ideas about what to do about gun violence but also facts and statistics to aid the argument in *50 Things You Can Do About Guns*. The first and possibly most sensible suggestion? If you have a gun in your home, get rid of it!"

> – **Publishers Weekly**
> March 28, 1994

The following poem, "Guns Are Fun", was written by John Hinckley. He bought a handgun from a Dallas, Texas dealer, without any background check whatsoever, and he used it to shoot Ronald Reagan.

Guns Are Fun

"See that living legend over there? With one little squeeze of the trigger I can put that person at my feet moaning and groaning and pleading with God. This gun gives me pornographic power. If I wish, the President will fall and the world will look at me in disbelief. All because I own an inexpensive gun."

50 THINGS YOU CAN DO ABOUT GUNS

By

James M. Murray

Robert D. Reed, Publishers • San Francisco, California

Robert D. Reed, Publishers
750 La Playa, Suite 647
San Francisco, CA 94121
Telephone: 1-800-PR-GREEN

Editing by Pamela D. Jacobs, M.A.
Typesetting by elletro Productions & PDJ
Cover by Joseph E. Haga

Published in cooperation with
CeaseFire, USA/Boston/San Francisco
Public Relations by Green-PR

Printed by Gilliland Printing
Distributed by Login Publishers Consortium
Telephone: (312) 733-8228 / Fax: (312) 733-3107

Library of Congress Cataloging-in-Publication Data

Murray, James M., 1946-
    50 things you can do about guns / by James M. Murray.
        p.   cm.
    ISBN 1-885003-00-5 : $7.95
    1. Gun control—United States. I. Title. II. Title: Fifty things you can do about guns.
    HV7436.M87   1994
    363.4'5'0973—dc20   94-17633
                                                          CIP

Dedication

For **Sean**...and for the future.

For my mother, **Isabella**, for her support and encouragement.

To the memory of **Kristin Lardner** and **Louis D. Brown**; and to all innocent victims of gunfire in America.

To a friend and fellow Vietnam veteran, Boston Police Detective **Thomas J. Gill**, who was killed in the line of duty in 1988 while investigating stolen guns.

J.M.M.

Contents

Acknowledgments

The Author wishes to thank a special group of Bostonians, known as the "**CeaseFire, Boston**" committee, for standing up for peace through democratic action and neighborhood involvement. They are: **Mark Bourbeau**, **Patsy Donovan**, **Craig Lankhorst**, **Dick McDonough** (who suggested the title for this book), **Andy Schell**, **Boyce Slayman**, **Jose Vincenty**, and **Tony Watson**. Also, "honorary members" **Jim Keeney** of Sturbridge and **Laurie Hall** of Reading, MA.

Thanks to Boston City Councilors, **Gareth Saunders** and **John Nucci**, for their assistance.

Thanks to **Citizens for Safety of Massachusetts**, especially Director **Katherine Mainzer** and **Michael McDonald**, for their help during the early stages of the CeaseFire referendum effort in Boston in 1992.

And a very special thanks to **Laura Brown** of the *Boston Herald*. She's a good friend of the truth and a **great** reporter.

A Special Word Of Thanks To My Publisher, Robert D. Reed

In all likelihood, *50 Things You Can Do About Guns* may not have seen the light of print if it were not for the vision and commitment to a better society of Robert (Bob) Reed and for some divine intervention.

So, what about Bob?

It seems as if Fate brought Bob and me into contact with each other to work toward our common goal of restoring peace in our society.

After finishing my manuscript, I wondered how in the world to find a publisher. I had no idea where to begin. Fortunately, my friend and neighbor, Sandy Storey (a published author and editor/publisher of my neighborhood newspaper), came to my rescue. She loaned me a book which lists alphabetically thousands of small, socially-responsible publishing houses throughout the United States.

I remember thinking that it could possibly take weeks to go through all of the listings. I decided to wait until the weekend when I would have more time to begin my search. Being curious, however, I opened the book somewhere near the middle, landing in the "R's". The first listing that I saw was California Publisher, Robert D. Reed.

As I was reviewing a thumbnail description of the types of books that Bob publishes, I felt that something "clicked" and I placed a bookmark on that page. After working my way through the entire book, I selected a number of other publishers to approach. However, Robert D. Reed was still at the top of my list.

After sending out my book proposal in December 1993, I heard from Bob within a week. I knew my search was over. Somehow it didn't matter to me if I received another offer from any other publisher because I knew that this was meant to be.

Living on opposite coasts, Bob and I began to communicate by phone and fax. He was enthusiastic and encouraging about my book. After mailing him my completed manuscript, he faxed me a contract within a week. Ours was, from the beginning, an informal, almost folksy, business relationship.

Since I don't have a fax machine at home (having only recently progressed to a color television and a touch-tone phone), I received his fax at the Photo Finish camera shop on Hanover Street in Boston's North End. There it was held in safekeeping for me by Kathy Granger, owner of the store and a good friend. The next morning I faxed the signed contract back to Bob and this book made a quantum leap from dream to reality.

From the start, I could tell that Bob and I were on the same wavelength. He seemed to understand what my book was all about. He agreed with me that it was important to make this book affordable and available to you.

Clearly, *50 Things You Can Do About Guns* was more than just another " book" to Bob, more than one more title of the many he has published during the past 28 years. Because he cares about people, Bob adopted this book as his "pet project," for which I am grateful.

We hope that after reading this book you will adopt one or more of the ideas presented herein; and that you will join us in our goal toward community safety and peace.

Jim Murray
Boston, MA
February 2, 1994

P.S. Finally, I met Bob and his partner, Pamela, while visiting the San Francisco Bay Area in April 1994. Besides being a great guy and a great publisher, Bob makes a great Boboli pizza. He and I have now formed **CeaseFire, USA** to encourage further anti-violence grassroots efforts.

Foreword

The purpose of this book is to help save lives and to make our communities safe again. I don't consider it to be the ultimate solution to the gun problem in America. I believe that **you**, the citizen, are the solution. This book is simply a tool that can help you.

Here are some reasons why we all must get involved:

1) Nearly one million people have been shot to death in America in this century.

2) More Americans have been killed by handguns in the last ten years alone than in Korea, Vietnam, and the Persian Gulf Wars combined.

3) There are more than 200 million guns in America and more gun dealers than gas stations in the U.S.

4) A handgun is manufactured every 20 seconds; and someone is shot in the U.S. every 20 seconds.

5) You are far more likely to be killed by a gun in your home than to be protected by it.

6) Every two hours a young person is shot in America. More than 200,000 people are injured by firearms in our country every year (30,000 of those shot die from the injuries).

7) Gunshot wounds add $14 billion to our health care costs every year.

It is no secret that guns and gun violence have become a national nightmare. Sadly, many Americans feel completely hopeless in dealing with this frightening situation. Many shrug and say, "People will always be able to get guns! So, what can we do?"

Plenty.

One person *can* make a difference, as John Kennedy once observed. However, people need information to "arm" themselves in the fight to rid their communities of the glut of guns. Gun violence has been threatening the very core of our society and disrupting our peace of mind. We all deserve to be safe and secure, whether at home, out in public places, in the workplace, or in the schools.

During the spring of 1992, in Boston, I joined with a small group of inner-city friends and neighbors to form a group called "**Cease-Fire**" (Citizens to Ensure a Safe Environment– Firearms Reduction Effort).

Our group was markedly different from some traditional "anti-gun" organizations. Avoiding rhetoric and sensationalism, we chose to educate ourselves about all facets of the gun problem, from local and state laws to Constitutional issues. In November 1992, we worked to place a referendum question regarding a ban on handguns in Boston on the ballot.

The question was worded in simple language and it was overwhelmingly approved by 62% of those who voted on it. The referendum carried in 81 out of 103 precincts where it appeared on the ballot in a cross-section of neighborhoods, representing Boston's ethnically and politically diverse communities.

CeaseFire raised no funds. We donated money from our own pockets to pay for photocopies, postage, and other expenses. We relied upon grassroots efforts to inform Bostonians that the non-binding referendum would be on the ballot. Citizens were told the truth about what the referendum could–and could not–do. Unfortunately, after the referendum was approved, gun violence has continued in Boston, particularly among young people (however, by no means, limited to them).

The following has also come to be:

> • Using the referendum results as documentation of the need for stronger gun measures in Boston, the City Council approved an ordinance banning the sale or possession of handguns to people under 21 years of age.

> • In the recent mayoral election, both finalists agreed to support a total ban on handguns in Boston, a position once deemed "political suicide". All candidates were briefed on the referendum and asked to take a strong position limiting handguns.

> • The Governor of Massachusetts (an ardent sportsman and previously considered to be strongly against gun restrictions) reversed his position almost 180 degrees. He submitted one of the most sweeping gun control packages in the nation to the state legislature.

I make no claims that the work of **CeaseFire** is directly responsible for any of the above initiatives. There are many other groups doing outstanding work in a variety of ways to deal with guns and violence. Still, in my mind, there is no question that **CeaseFire** has influenced greatly these developments by working on a grassroots level to provide objective information through community education combined with civic action.

Though the referendum was the focal point of our efforts, we worked with other groups involved with different facets of the gun problem. Working on the community level taught us a great deal. Still there is much to learn about the nature of gun violence in our city and our country.

In this book, I have attempted to pare down a massive amount of material that I have studied and collected over the years. I have included knowledge gained through the **CeaseFire** experience. This concise, readable "citizen's guide" offers 50 tangible and practical things that individuals and community groups can do to empower themselves. Positive civic action can help to make our communities safer places in which to live, work, and visit.

I've included support materials, such as: information pertaining to the truth about The Second Amendment and the "right to bear arms," press clips, and "letters to the editor" (to both daily and weekly neighborhood newspapers). These materials, based on the work and success of **CeaseFire**, **Boston**, may encourage readers to create their own programs and show them how to take action.

Books are copyrighted but ideas are not. Please feel free to use any ideas that you find helpful and send me **your** ideas as well.

J.M.M.
April 1994

50 THINGS YOU CAN DO ABOUT GUNS

1 If You Have A Gun In Your Home, Consider Getting Rid Of It!

Guns in the home for self protection are 43 times more likely to kill a family member or friend than an intruder, according to the *New England Journal of Medicine*, June 1986.

Also, consider this...

- Individuals armed with handguns committed a record 930,700 violent crimes in 1992 and set a record of 917,500 for use of handguns in nonfatal crimes, almost 50 percent higher than the average for the previous five years. Handgun homicides reached 13,200 in 1992, a 24 percent increase over the previous five-year average. (Highlights of the Justice Department's report on handguns. *San Francisco Chronicle.* May 16, 1994.)

- In 1991, there were only 240 "justifiable" handgun homicides compared with a total of 12,090 handgun murders in the United States (not counting suicides and accidental shootings).

- About one million people have been shot to death in America in this century alone. More than 30,000 Americans die from guns every year. Another 200,000 are injured, many horribly wounded—for life.

- There are an estimated 200 million firearms in the possession of private citizens in the United States (and this estimate is conservative). Since firearms are not "biodegradable", they tend to change hands many times during their long "shelf life". There are nearly as many guns in America as there are people. Perhaps more.

- According to *USA Today*, in 1990, handgun murder rates around the world were as follows:

Sweden	13
Switzerland	91
Japan	87
Canada	68
Great Britain	22
Australia	10
United States	**10,567**

- A handgun is manufactured every 20 seconds in the United States; and a person is shot every 20 seconds in the United States.

- About two million handguns are manufactured and imported into the U.S. each year.

CHILDREN
AND
GUNS

2 If You Insist Upon Keeping A Gun In Your Home, Be Sure It Is Secure And Out Of The Reach Of Children!

The state of Florida, requires gun owners to lock and secure their guns where there are children in the home. The 1989 statute, called the Child Accident Prevention Law, was the basis for prosecuting a Jacksonville couple in 1992, after their 2 year old daughter was shot by her 3 year old brother. The couple kept a loaded Magnum revolver under their mattress and a loaded semiautomatic pistol on the headboard of their bed.

In Connecticut, a 5 year old boy shot himself, sustaining serious head and chest wounds when he was struck by a single bullet from a 9mm automatic pistol. The boy's mother was talking on the telephone when she heard the shot.

- More than 1.2 million elementary-age, latchkey children have access to guns in their homes.

- Every day twelve children are shot to death in America. Many more are wounded.

- The incidence of suicide is five times higher where a gun is in the home. In cities such as Boston, 60% of the teenagers who commit suicide use a gun found in the home.

- Every six hours a youth (from age 10-19) commits suicide with a gun in America.

- In 1991, 1/6 of all pediatricians in the U.S. reported having treated a child with a gunshot wound.

3 If You Have Friends, Relatives, Or Acquaintances Who Keep Guns In The Home...

Ask them to keep their guns locked away from young children. Be firm in voicing your concern!

4 If Gunowner Friends Do Not Keep Their Guns Locked Up...

And out of reach of young children, don't allow your children to visit that house—under any circumstances!

5 Lobby Your State Legislature...

And/or local government for a state law or city ordinance similar to that of Florida's Child Accident Prevention Law. This Law requires that gunowners lock and secure their guns where there are children in the home. Organize a petition drive or local referendum on the matter.

6 Recognize That, Increasingly, Children Are Becoming Gun Victims In The U.S.

In 1987, researchers found that the King/Drew Medical Center in Los Angeles hadn't admitted a single child under age 10 for gunshot wounds before 1980. However, from 1980 to 1987, the center admitted 34 young children.

7 Again, If You Insist Upon Keeping A Gun In The Home, *Don't* Make It A Handgun.

Handguns are made for one purpose—to kill people.

Every year, more than 24,000 Americans are killed with handguns—in murders, suicides and accidents. That's as many as are killed annually by drunk drivers. That's 65 American men, women and children every day.

Handguns have become cheap, readily available, easily concealable and, with new technology, far more lethal in terms of firepower. In October of 1991, in Killeen, Texas, a man crashed his pickup truck through the window of a crowded cafeteria and, within minutes, killed 23 people and wounded several others with just two 9mm automatic pistols.

Handguns are the favorite targets of burglars who almost always strike when no one is at home. Within weeks, the stolen gun will end up on the streets to be used in crime. 500,000 guns are stolen in the U.S. every year, most of them handguns. Forty per cent of guns used in crimes are stolen guns.

In 1990, 65 law enforcement officers were killed in the line of duty—48 with handguns.

U.S. Department of justice figures reveal that handguns, in addition to killing more than 24,000 Americans every year, are used in more than 600,000 violent crimes in America annually. Every 24 hours, 33 women are raped, 575 people are robbed, and 1,116 people are assaulted by handgun-wielding assailants.

Handgun Facts

- Handguns were used to murder 13,200 people in this country in 1992—a 24% increase over the previous five-year average.

- Every year, more than 24,000 Americans are killed with handguns—in homicides, suicides and accidents; as many as are killed annually by drunk drivers. That's 65 American men, women and children every day!

- 11,152 Americans took their lives with handguns in 1989.

- Each year, about 1500 people are accidentally killed with guns.

- Every day, 12 children, aged 19 and under, are killed with guns. Many more are injured.

- There are an estimated 200 million firearms in the possession of private citizens in the U.S.

- 60-70 million of the firearms in circulation are handguns.

- The government keeps no specific records on assault weapons. However, the Bureau of Alcohol, Tobacco and Firearms estimates there are one million semiautomatic assault weapons in private hands in the U.S.

- A new handgun is produced every 20 seconds. Every 2 minutes, a handgun injures someone.

- At least $1 billion is spent annually on hospital costs associated with the treatment of individuals who have been shot.

- Firearm injuries result in $14.4 billion in lifetime costs per year. Lifetime costs include medical costs and loss of productivity.

- Every six hours, a youth (from age 10-19) commits suicide with a gun. In 1989, nearly 1,400 youths were killed this way.

- In 1990, 65 law enforcement officers were killed in the line of duty, 48 with handguns.

- In 1990, handguns were used to murder 13 people in Sweden, 91 in Switzerland, 87 in Japan, 68 in Canada, 22 in Great Britain, 10 in Australia, and 10,567 in the United States.

- In 1989, according to the FBI Uniform Crime Reports, there were only 178 justifiable handgun homicides by private citizens in the United States.

- According to the U.S. Department of Justice, "Offenders armed with handguns committed an average of 639,000 violent crimes each year between 1979 and 1987." Violent crimes are murders, rapes, robberies and assaults.

8 Restrict Your Children's Television Time.

Studies have shown that the average child will witness more than 100,000 murders on television by the time that he or she reaches the age of eighteen. Violence on television, many times graphically but rarely realistically portrayed, gives a child the impression that death and injury is "not real". It detaches them from the grim reality of pain and suffering and grief of "real" violence. One New York City youth, incarcerated for the shooting death of another boy, described the experience as "like watching a movie" as he gunned down his victim.

Television ads can be equally as harmful as the violence portrayed in TV shows, particularly beer commercials which are increasingly aimed at a younger market and appear to be airing more than ever before. Also the emphasis upon material things such as cars and clothing more often than not raise expectations and a desire to "have it all" among impressionable youngsters. The ads rarely point to the work and sacrifice required in obtaining many of these possessions and the unlikelihood that many viewers will be able to afford them, particularly in a slow economy. The ads merely create the demand so that the consumer will buy the product and reduce the supply and create more demand. Where and how the money is obtained to consume the products appears not to be a factor in the production and airing of the ads.

9 Demand A Violence Prevention Program And Curriculum For Your Child's School That Includes A Component On Guns.

Considering that the national juvenile homicide rate has doubled between 1983 and 1993, violence prevention programs are an absolute must in the classroom today. Every state establishes basic curriculum requirements for the local school districts which are often updated to reflect changing developments in society, such as AIDS prevention education. Violence has become no less epidemic in America and the classroom (as well as the home) is the obvious and proper setting for violence prevention education.

With the prevalence of guns in American society, a curriculum dealing with violence must include a section on guns. And gun violence is not limited to homicide. As noted, earlier, many children die in gun-related accidents and in suicides. According to the Center for Disease Control, the suicide rate for youngsters between 15 and 19 quadrupled between 1950 and 1988. 65 per cent of teenage males and 47 per cent of female teens who commit suicide use a gun according to the National Center for Health Statistics.

There are specialized curricula available such as the "STAR" program ("Straight Talk About Risks"), developed by the Center to Prevent Handgun Violence (The group headed by Sarah Brady that led the movement to enact passage of the handgun waiting period legislation known as "The Brady Bill".)

The STAR program, according to the Center, is "the nation's only pre-K through 12th-grade school program designed to teach children how to stay safe when encountering guns, how to resist peer pressure to play with or carry guns, and how to distinguish between real life and TV violence". The STAR program also deals with conflict resolution without violence. For more information, contact:

Center to Prevent Handgun Violence
1225 Eye Street, NW, Room 1150
Washington, DC 20005
(202) 289-7319

Parents, teachers, law enforcement officials, youth agencies and health care workers would make an ideal coalition for pressing local schools to adopt the STAR program or a similar program which addresses violence in general and gun violence in particular.

10 Don't Tolerate Guns In Your Child's School!

An estimated one million latchkey children of elementary school age have access to a gun in the home. An estimated 200,000 children are bringing guns to school on an average school day in America. Often they are very young, some barely in their teens. One 6 year old was found with a gun in a school in Florida. An estimated 160,000 children stay home from school every day because they are afraid.

Many schools are now equipped with metal detectors, which certainly help. But many school codes have not been updated in terms of the reality of the 1990s and still treat the carrying of a gun by a student as a behavioral infraction instead of the deadly business that it is. Carrying a gun into a school is not akin to chewing gum in class or skipping out at last period. Expulsion, even for a "first offense" is the only answer to discouraging the bringing of a gun to school. This may seem harsh to some child advocates, but the mainstream of students must be protected from the potential of violence and the fear that guns in a school can bring.

Find out what your local school policy is regarding guns brought into your child's school. If the policy is weak and lacking in protection for your child and teachers you may get together with other parents and demand that the school's policy be upgraded for today's realities. Your child has a right to peace of mind and personal safety in the classroom and throughout the school.

11 Do Not Give Toy Guns As Gifts.

Sociologists may argue about the relationship between violence and the use of toy guns by children, but clearly in today's society there is no need to promote and encourage the use of toy weapons as playthings. They only serve to reinforce the notion of our society as one of a "gun-culture" and the act of an adult in giving a child a toy gun as a birthday gift or holiday present only serves to validate that notion for a child.

One inner city youth program received a donation of toys for their annual Christmas party for local children. Included in the shipment was a number of toy pistols and assault weapons. The program director told me that she called the donor and asked that the toy guns be picked up. She would not be distributing them to the children with whom she worked. "We really don't need any more guns in our community—toy guns or otherwise", she told me.

12 Practice "Toy Gun Control" In Your Home.

In spite of your best efforts, you may find toy guns cropping up all over your home. Kids receive them as gifts or often buy them with their own money. It happened in my own home where I grew tired of having a toy pistol stuck in my face at dinner and finally put my foot down. No toy guns were allowed outside my son's room except for the back yard where he and his friends could play with them all they pleased. I felt it important for him to know that there were limits to guns, even toy guns, and that some adults did not embrace the gun culture.

13 Monitor Home Videos For Gun-Oriented Promotions And Contests.

I was recently startled to learn that one "action" home video featuring a well-known "action hero" contained a lead-in detailing a contest for young children who could win prizes by correctly naming certain types of automatic handguns and assault weapons that were displayed on the screen. There is no need for paying good money to rent a movie so that gun dealers and manufacturers can "preview" their wares for a new generation of potential customers. Let your video rental store know that you don't approve of these videos with built-in "commercials" for guns should you find similar contests and promotions when you or your children rent a video.

14 Object To Gun And Violence Oriented Video Game Commercials.

Many of today's video games are violence-centered. One such ad contains a "live-action" clip of a woman being kicked in the stomach. It may be an individual choice to purchase or rent these violent electronic games, but advertising them on the public air waves is another story. Television stations are licensed by the Federal Communications Commission to operate in the public interest, which clearly is not served by promoting violence. The air waves belong to you, the citizen. You are, in effect the "landlord", as Ralph Nader has pointed out. The television stations are the "tenant". If you are bothered by the promotion and glorification of violence, particularly as geared toward your children, let your local television station and Congressional representatives know how you feel.

Speak out!

15 Talk To Young Children About The Reality of Gunshot Wounds And Death.

Violence in movies and television is, of course, greatly sugar-coated and "sanitized", far removed from harsh reality. People who are shot in movies and television do not go into immediate shock or cardiac arrest as do real life victims, even from minor wounds. They don't cry for their mothers or empty their bladders and bowels as do real life victims. They don't scream and moan or cry out in pain. If wounded, they merely hold their hands to the wound as if they had suffered a bee sting. If killed, they simply fall quietly to the ground.

It is not fun to be shot and not a pretty sight when it happens. Young people need to know the reality of the shock and trauma to the human body and mind—both of which are scarred (often forever) when a person is shot.

Of course some children may not be up to learning about the real effects of gunshot wounds, a parent would have to make an individual decision about that. As a young person has no sense of reality about what guns can actually do, he may be less inhibited about pulling a trigger on another human being, on another child.

"Non-authority" figures such as veterans would be excellent speakers for a program designed to teach children the reality of getting shot in a society that is increasingly beginning to resemble a war zone.

16 Teach Your Children What To Do If They Should Find A Gun.

With the number of guns out there, it is not beyond the realm of possibility that he or she could come across a gun that has been "stashed" or discarded following a crime. It happened with my own son who was 13 at the time. Someone had tossed or hidden a pistol and some rounds in the shrubbery in the front yard in our urban neighborhood. Fortunately an adult was present and the police were notified and quickly responded to remove it.

A child should be taught to consider every gun as loaded and to treat it the same way as a strange dog or a live wire. The first rule in those situations should and must be, **"Do Not Touch!"** Secondly, find a grown-up and/or call 911 immediately.

17 If You Know Of A Child With A Gun, Notify Authorities Immediately.

No one wants to get a child into trouble or be seen as an informer. However, if you know of a child with a gun that means your own children could be in danger. Notify authorities. You don't have to give your name. Some police departments have "hot lines" just for that purpose. In some regions, the Federal Alcohol, Tobacco and Firearms Bureau (ATF) has a special toll-free number (1-800 ATF-GUNS) for reporting illegal guns. Call for help, as your child's life and safety are at stake.

18 Organize A "Toy Gun Buy-Back" Program In Your Community.

As discussed later in this book, many cities and towns across America are seeing gun "buy-back" programs being established by community and antiviolence groups. Citizens who want to get rid of guns from their home have an opportunity to do so, voluntarily. They may be given modest compensation in return for their unwanted guns.

Cities such as Omaha, however, have carried the "buy-back" idea a step forward to include toy guns where children may "sell" their toy guns for one dollar per toy gun. Other cities have adopted similar programs where books or games are given in return for the toy weapons.

The idea being, of course, to discourage the continuance of the gun culture in our society and to offer children alternative and positive means of recreation.

Toy gun buy-back programs are relatively easy to organize and have been met with enthusiasm by the best possible population, the children themselves. Libraries, youth centers, schools, and recreational centers have proven to be popular sites for the toy gun turn-ins. Donations to cover costs come from a variety of sources, including local businesses, charitable organizations and individual contributions from neighborhood residents.

WOMEN
AND
GUNS

Women And Guns

Guns in the home for self-protection are 43 times more likely to kill a family member or friend than to kill an intruder.
(Study by Arthur Kellerman, et al, *The New England Journal of Medicine*, June 1986.)

In 1991, there were only 240 justifiable handgun homicides compared with a total of 12,090 handgun murders in the U.S.
(FBI Uniform Crime Reports)

Every day, 12 American children are killed with guns.
(National Center for Health Statistics)

Domestic handgun production rose steadily through the mid-1970s, peaking in 1982, and then it declined through the mid-1980s. It began climbing again in 1987. In 1990, 1,818,627 handguns were produced by domestic manufacturers for private sale in the U.S.
(Bureau of Alcohol, Tobacco and Firearms Production Data)

"When gun production goes down, promotion to women goes up."
(Marketing to Women Newsletter, November 1987)

"There simply are too many manufacturers for a shrinking or stagnant market—the industry needs to find new markets to survive and prosper."
(American Rifleman, published by the NRA, March 1989)

"One of the quickest ways to boost firearm sales is to inform the public that you are offering women the same fun shooting opportunities as the men."
(American Firearms Industry magazine, October 1990)

More than 1.2 million elementary-aged, latchkey children have access to guns in their homes.
(Centers for Disease Control)
(Courtesy: Citizens for Safety, Massachusetts)

With the astronomical number of gun deaths and injuries of women and children, a new "market" for women has sprung up almost overnight. There are an estimated 15 million women who possess handguns in the U.S. and the number appears to be growing. With the glut of the male market for guns which unquestionably has been a prime factor in the rise of female fatalities and shootings, an aggressive campaign is underway to convince American women that their only protection from rapists, muggers, murderers and criminals is a gun. In some rare instances, this may, in fact, be true. But every citizen, male or female, should consider all of the ramifications of securing a firearm and be absolutely sure that a gun will not be used against them, end up in the wrong hands, or cause a tragedy in the home.

As noted, studies have shown that a gun in the home is far more likely to be misused than to provide personal protection for the owner.

A first-of-its-kind study by the Harvard School of Public Health in 1993 provided conclusive evidence that having a gun in the home nearly triples the odds that someone in the house will be murdered, usually by a family or close friend. The study, which was conducted by Dr. Arthur Kellerman of the Emory Center for Injury Prevention, examined hundreds of households in three states Tennessee, Ohio and Washington in which people had been killed. Their findings, which were published in the *New England Journal of Medicine* in October, 1993, revealed that a majority occurred within the context of a romantic dispute or an argument. 76.7 per cent of the victims were killed by a family member or an acquaintance.

Clearly, arming one's self is a decision that should not be made lightly. There are many serious implications in gun ownership.

19 Ask Yourself If You Are Fully Prepared To Use A Gun On Someone.

Purchasing a gun, even after a waiting period and background check, many prove to be the easiest part of owning and carrying a firearm. However, using the gun in a tense and frightening situation (with only a split-second to make a judgment while the adrenaline is flowing) may prove far more difficult. Even seasoned law enforcement professionals who undergo regular training can make mistakes in dangerous situations. It is not easy to kill someone, even in life threatening situations. Be sure that once you draw a weapon, you are positive that your life or other lives are in danger; and that you are prepared to kill the person who poses the threat. There is no other way to say it. If you are not fully prepared to use your gun, then get rid of it. Otherwise you are inviting tragedy, especially if an assailant has a gun of his own.

20 If You Choose Against Carrying A Gun, Consider Alternative Means Of Self-Protection.

People, especially women who have become increasingly vulnerable to crime and personal attacks, have a right to protect themselves. This can take many forms. But the main form of self protection is *escape* from a potential threat to your safety.

21 If You Are The Victim Of A Mugging, Do Not Resist.

It may seem like "giving in" to criminals not to put up a fight to protect your valuables, but nothing you own is worth your life. In a society where people are now routinely being shot for no reason at all, it is foolhardy to think that you would not be shot for your money or jewelry. Keeping yourself safe must be your main priority.

22 If Someone Gets Into Your Car, Get Out And Run.

NEVER stay in a vehicle or get into one, even if ordered to do so at gun point. In a situation like that, your best option is to *run.* There is risk involved, unquestionably, but once you get into a car with a potential assailant your personal risk increases greatly. Try to run in the opposite direction from which the car is facing. This may give you more of a chance to escape since the attacker would be forced to back up or get out of the vehicle to chase you.

Chances are reasonably good that an attacker may not shoot as you flee. Chances are equally good that he will not hit you, especially with a handgun. And chances are fairly good that should you be wounded, it will not be fatal. Measured against your chances of survival (should you stay in your car or get into an assailant's vehicle to be taken to a more secluded area), taking flight is a better option. Screaming for help and bringing attention to your situation may save your life.

This suggestion was offered by a police detective on a television show about self-defense for women.

23 Consider Chemical Repellents As An Alternative To A Gun.

Chemical sprays, such as "Mace" or pepper sprays, have proven to be effective in repelling attackers and aiding escape. Some states require that you have training and/or a license to carry these devices. Be sure to check with local law enforcement authorities before arming yourself.

The advantages of Mace-like sprays are many. A spray can be carried conveniently in a purse or coat pocket without fear that it will go off by accident or cause serious injury as would a handgun. A chemical spray can be carried in the hand as you enter your car or home without the chilling effect of carrying a handgun. More concealable than a handgun, it is more discreet.

Best of all, chemical sprays are nonlethal and there is little conscience-wrestling involved in their use. They are designed for "close-up" use, when you are most sure that there is a threat to you. There is little danger of shooting the wrong person from a few feet away. Most importantly, even if your canister is taken away from you, unlike a handgun, it cannot be used to wound or kill you.

This is not to say that a chemical spray is absolutely safe. Caution and prudence *must* be exercised because it is still a weapon, albeit a nonlethal defensive one. Great care must be taken to keep such sprays out of the hands of children. Used properly, they can help a potential victim *escape* from a dangerous situation.

24 Practice Good Security At Home.

As an alternative to a gun in the home be sure that your house is as secure as possible.

New technology has allowed for relatively inexpensive alarm and detection systems, including motion detectors that will automatically activate exterior lighting. Be sure that your locks are durable and high-quality. Make all doors and windows as "burglar-proof" as possible. Your local police department can help to advise you on how to make your home secure.

25 Do Not Open Your Door To A Stranger, Especially If You Are Home Alone.

At one time Americans did not lock their doors and they had no fear of a stranger's knock. This is not the case today.

In a time of increasing "home invasions" opening one's door (especially at night to someone unknown to us) can invite tragedy. It is hard for most of us to refuse to help a stranger in need. However the risks have become too great, especially for women living alone.

26 If You Feel In Danger In Any Way While At Home, Call 911.

Nearly 40% of 911 calls in Boston are of a frivolous nature (e.g. "Has the Red Sox game been postponed?" or "What time do the Pops go on at the Esplanade?"). Sadly, many calls that the police should receive are never made. If you hear a strange noise inside or outside of your home, call the police. Don't be afraid of being embarrassed should your fears prove groundless. One of their duties is to come to your home and check things out. "Better safe than sorry" may sound trite, but it is true.

27 Take Precautions In The Workplace.

Increasingly, the workplace is becoming a dangerous place for both men and women, but not just because of industrial accidents. (See "The Violent Workplace" chart, page 39).

In New York City, for example, the greatest single cause of death in the workplace has become homicide, usually by a handgun.

Likewise in Massachusetts where, for the first time, homicide has become the leading cause of death in the workplace, primarily due to robbery attempts.

Nationally, the major cause of death for women in the workplace has been murder, the result not only of crime but of domestic-related violence. Now men find themselves equally at risk, particularly those working in high-risk occupations such as convenience store clerks and taxi drivers.

Arming one's self may give a person a sense of security, unfortunately a false one. In most cases, it simply invites tragedy in the form of accidents, suicide, being disarmed and then shot with a person's own weapon, or having the gun stolen.

Many workers' groups and labor unions are pushing for strengthening of federal and state workplace safety laws in light of the latest trend of murders in workplaces.

Exercise great caution when working in a high risk position, such as any job where cash is handled routinely. Demand better safeguards in terms of protective windows, secure work areas, adequate security lighting, staffing and on-site security guards with communication links to the local law enforcement agencies for providing rapid response.

With so many guns out in our communities now, and so many people willing to use them without a moment's hesitation, keep your own well-being your top priority.

Money is the last thing in the world for which to die.

The violent workplace

Reasons for the violence

American workers believe drug use, layoffs and poverty are the major reasons for on-the-job violence.

Alcohol and drug abuse **59%**

Layoffs/firings **53%**

Poverty **52%**

Availability of guns **46%**

Violence on TV or in movies **36%**

Pressure/ Too much work **34%**

Overly controlling management **32%**

Conflicts with co-workers **28%**

Deadly jobs

Here is the homicide rate for every 100,000 workers between 1980-88:

Laborer **1.56**

Transport operator **1.53**

Sales **1.38**

Service **1.00**

Executive/ Administrative/ Manager **0.92**

Farmers **0.49**

Crafts **0.42**

Professional **0.27**

Machine operator **0.20**

Clerical **0.19**

Technical support **0.12**

Culprits

Who is the attacker?

Customer **44%**

Stranger **24%**

Co-worker **20%**

Boss **7%**

Former employee **3%**

Other **3%**

Who is the harasser?

Co-worker **47%**

Boss **39%**

Customer **15%**

Stranger **2%**

Former employee **2%**

Other **2%**

Sources: "Fear and Violence in the Workplace" study, Northwestern National Life Insurance Co., John Hancock Jr., Detroit attorney, Census of Fatal Occupational Injuries, Michigan Department of Labor, "Violence in the Workplace," S. Anthony Baron and workplace violence experts and studies

The Detroit News

28 Exercise Great Care During Hunting Season.

Inebriated hunters shooting helpless cows and sometimes each other or themselves are often the butt of jokes in our society. Increasingly that stereotype is beginning to emerge as more fact than fiction. Some areas report that more people are killed than deer. Each year brings more "horror stories" of people being shot while jogging, playing in the yard, or hanging out their wash to dry during hunting season. Wearing bright colors or shouting warnings to hunters is having no effect. More and more innocent people are being shot as they are "mistaken for deer".

Guns kill as many people in America every day as do drunk drivers. Perhaps the time has come to treat "drunk hunters" with equal severity. If someone is in a wooded area, under the influence of alcohol, within range of people's homes, that is no less a threat to public safety than if that same hunter were careening down the highway at 90 miles per hour. In that situation, the police would be sure to pursue and arrest him, locking him up as a menace to other motorists. They should do no less for the hunter who is intoxicated. There is no humor in being shot by a deer slug while sitting in your backyard.

Those living in hunting areas during "season" have learned to remain indoors as much as possible and to keep their children inside. Even responsible hunters, who exercise care and control, should understand that society has changed greatly, especially in the great outdoors.

Early in 1993, a man was arrested on firearms charges by federal agents in Ohio in connection with the apparently motiveless murders of five hunters in that state in a three year period. The agents had followed a man who spent weekends drinking, cruising lonely roads, shooting at road signs and poles, and killing more than 1,000 animals, mostly cats, dogs and cattle. The suspect told investigators that he owned as many as 500 guns. Authorities are investigating several other deaths of sportsmen in neighboring states that were originally believed to be hunting accidents.

GUNS
AND YOUR
COMMUNITY

29 Find Out About Your Local Gun Permit Laws And Regulations. Ask Questions.

Keep in mind that the U.S. Supreme Court has ruled consistently that the Second Amendment "right to bear arms" is not binding upon the states and that state and local governments may enact any gun regulatory measures they see fit. Find out what laws pertain to guns in your community.

Ask questions ...

- What are the procedures, requirements and regulations for owning and/or carrying a gun in your city or town?
- Who is the licensing authority? Who is responsible for the issuance of gun permits?
- How long are permits good for? What is the renewal procedure?
- Are minors permitted to obtain handgun permits and under what circumstances? Is parental approval required?
- Are gun owners, especially handgun owners, required to bring their guns in for inspection at regular intervals to prove that the gun is still in the possession of the legal owner?
- What are the penalties in your city, town or state for carrying an unlicensed firearm?

- What are the penalties for illegally selling a legally obtained firearm to an individual not legally able to obtain a gun?
- What is the policy concerning licensed gun owners who have had restraining orders taken out against them for domestic abuse? Is the gun automatically subject to confiscation by the police? Under what conditions will the gun be returned?
- Is there an "early warning system" to detect a potential threat to a victim of domestic violence or abuse where a gun is in the home?
- Are gun ownership records routinely checked in cases of suspected wife-battering and domestic abuse and violence?
- How many permits and licenses for private citizens to carry guns exist in your city or town? How many are issued every year?

The above questions are important ones when considering the alarming increase in domestic violence in America and the increasing number of "legal" guns ending up in the hands of people who are not legally qualified to possess them.

- In 1991, a Springfield, Massachusetts man shot three people to death, including a pregnant woman and an 8 year old boy. The individual's Firearm Identification Card, which he had since the age of 15, had never been revoked, in spite of a felony conviction.

- In a case that captured national headlines in 1989, Charles Stuart was seriously wounded and his pregnant wife shot to death in Boston in what he said was a robbery attempt. Stuart later apparently committed suicide when questions arose about the incident and evidence came to light that his wounds may have been self-inflicted and he may have shot his wife. The handgun used in the shootings was found to be the property of his employer, a Boston furrier, who thought that the gun was in his safe, at his place of business.

- Half a million guns are stolen each year in America. Although about half of them are recovered by police, the remainder leave a deadly toll of gunshot wounds and deaths.

- In Arizona, a loophole in state law makes it legal for anyone of any age to openly carry firearms anywhere they please, even though the number of Arizona children arrested for violent crime has risen from 976 in 1987 to 2,093 in 1991. The crimes included murder, rape, robbery and aggravated assault. Local Arizona cities and towns are adopting their own ordinances to address the situation, including Phoenix which saw 1,200 incidents of aggravated assaults committed by armed juveniles in 1991. The new local ordinance requires parental approval in writing before a minor may carry a firearm. Although the ordinance may not appear that far-reaching, it does point out the initiative of a local community in taking action when state laws are too lax or have not been amended to reflect the epidemic of gun violence in today's society.

The Second Amendment

FACT:

No gun control measure has ever been struck down as unconstitutional under the Second Amendment.

30 Did You Know That No Gun Control Law Has Ever Been Struck Down As Unconstitutional Under The Second Amendment? Learn About The Myth And Reality Of The "Right To Bear Arms."

The Second Amendment reads:

> A well regulated Militia, being necessary to the security of a free State, the right of the people to keep and bear Arms, shall not be infringed.

No one would deny a citizen the right of self-protection, but there is no absolute right of an individual to own or carry a firearm in the United States. The origin of the Second Amendment may be found in its first line which speaks of a "well-regulated militia", i.e. the National Guard. Many of the founders of our country who helped to frame the Constitution feared the power of a strong central government, having just fought a long and hard battle for independence against Great Britain.

The Second Amendment was included to guarantee the right of a *state* to "keep and bear arms" to protect it's sovereignty. It was *not* intended to guarantee *individuals* a right to a gun.

Six U.S. Supreme Court decisions and more than forty lower court decisions have reaffirmed that there is no right of an individual to own a gun from "Presser v. Illinois" 1886, to "United States v. Miller", 1939 to the ban on handguns imposed by the village of Morton Grove, Illinois in 1982. This law was upheld by the 7th Circuit Court and the Supreme Court refused to review it.

In spite of much misinformation and misinterpretation of the Second Amendment (see following pages) by some individuals, groups and the gun lobby, the "right to bear arms" belongs to the state, not to the individual.

GUNS AND THE 2nd AMENDMENT TO THE U.S. CONSTITUTION

A well regulated Militia being necessary to the security of a free State, the right of the people to keep and bear Arms shall not be infringed.
-- Second Amendment to the U.S. Constitution

The Second Amendment does not provide an individual right to carry a gun. No federal court has ever overturned a gun control law on the grounds that it violates the Second Amendment to the U.S. Constitution.

WARREN E. BURGER -- *RET. CHIEF JUSTICE OF THE U.S. SUPREME COURT*

"Few things have been more vigorously debated -- and distorted -- in recent times than the meaning of [the Second Amendment]... few subjects have been as cluttered and confused by calculated disinformation circulated by special interest groups.

"To really understand what was intended, it is necessary to look back and recall that in those days people had a great fear of a standing national army... The real purpose of the Second Amendment was to ensure that the 'state armies' -- 'the militia' -- would be maintained for the defense of the state... The very language of the Second Amendment refutes any argument that it was intended to guarantee every citizen an unfettered right to any kind of weapon he or she desires. In referring to 'a well regulated militia,' the Framers clearly intended to secure the right to bear arms essentially for military purposes...

"That there should be vigorous debate on this subject is a tribute to our freedom of speech and press, but the American people should have a firm understanding of the true origin and purpose of the Second Amendment." (11/26/91, Keene Sentinel)

ERWIN N. GRISWOLD -- *SOLICITOR GENERAL, NIXON ADMINISTRATION*

"[Gun lobby] lawmakers and their mentors in the National Rifle Association should recognize the undeniable fact that the Second Amendment has never been an impediment to laws limiting private ownership of firearms... The clear meaning of [the Supreme Court's 1939 opinion in *United States v. Miller*] is that the Constitution does not guarantee a right to be armed for private purposes unrelated to the organized state militia...

"Following the Supreme Court's lead, the lower federal courts have shown remarkable unanimity in applying the Second Amendment. Never in history has a federal court invalidated a law regulating the private ownership of firearms on Second Amendment grounds. Indeed, that the Second Amendment poses no barrier to strong gun laws is perhaps the most well-settled proposition in American constitutional law. Yet the incantation of this phantom right continues to pervade congressional debate..." (11/4/90, Washington Post)

Courtesy, Office of U.S. Senator John Chafee

U.S. COURTS OF APPEALS ON THE 2nd AMENDMENT

Stevens v. United States, 1971   (6th Circuit)
"Since the Second Amendment right 'to keep and bear arms' applies only to the right of the State to maintain a militia and not to the individual's right to bear arms, there can be no serious claim to any express constitutional right of an individual to possess a firearm."

United States v. Synnes, 1971   (8th Circuit)
"[W]e decide only that the right to bear arms is not the type of fundamental right to which the 'compelling state interest' standard attaches... Although Sec. 1202(a) is the broadest federal gun legislation to date, we see no conflict between it and the Second Amendment since there is no showing that prohibiting possession of firearms by felons obstructs the maintenance of a 'well regulated militia.'"

Eckert v. City of Philadelphia, 1973   (3rd Circuit)
"Appellant's theory in the district court which he now repeats is that by the Second Amendment to the United States Constitution he is entitled to bear arms. Appellant is completely wrong about that... It must be remembered that the right to keep and bear arms is not a right given by the United States Constitution."

United States v. Johnson, 1974   (4th Circuit)
"The courts have consistently held that the Second Amendment only confers a collective right of keeping and bearing arms which must bear a 'reasonable relationship to the preservation or efficiency of a well regulated militia.'"

United States v. Warin, 1976   (6th Circuit)
"It is clear that the Second Amendment guarantees a collective rather than an individual right... It would unduly extend this opinion to attempt to deal with every argument... based on the erroneous supposition that the Second Amendment is concerned with the rights of individuals rather than those of the States..."

Quilici v. Village of Morton Grove, 1982   (7th Circuit)
"Construing [the language of the Second Amendment] according to its plain meaning, it seems clear that the right to bear arms is inextricably connected to the preservation of a militia... we conclude that the right to keep and bear handguns is not guaranteed by the second amendment."

Courtesy, Office of U.S. Senator John Chafee

U.S. SUPREME COURT ON THE 2nd AMENDMENT

U.S. v. Miller, 1939

"In the absence of any evidence tending to show that possession or use of a [shotgun] at this time has some reasonable relationship to the preservation or efficiency of a well regulated militia, we cannot say that the Second Amendment guarantees the right to keep and bear such an instrument... With obvious purpose to assure the continuation and render possible the effectiveness of such forces the declaration and guarantee of the Second Amendment were made. It must be interpreted and applied with that end in view."

Burton v. Sills, 1969

Dismissed for want of a substantial federal question an appeal from the Supreme Court of New Jersey, which stated:

"As the language of the [U.S. Constitution's Second] Amendment itself indicates it was not framed with individual rights in mind. Thus it refers to the collective right "of the people" to keep and bear arms in connection with "a well-regulated militia"... [most agree this term] must be taken to mean the active, organized militia of each state, which today is characterized as the state National Guard... Reasonable gun control legislation is clearly within the police power of the State and must be accepted by the individual though it may impose a restraint or burden on him."

Lewis v. United States, 1980

"These legislative restrictions on the use of firearms are neither based upon constitutionally suspect criteria, nor do they trench upon any constitutionally protected liberties...the Second Amendment guarantees no right to keep and bear a firearm that does not have 'some reasonable relationship to the preservation or efficiency of a well regulated militia.'"

Courtesy, Office of U.S. Senator John Chafee

31 Find Out What Becomes Of Confiscated Guns In Your Community.

Most cities and towns routinely destroy guns that are confiscated in criminal cases but some local officials have been selling them to gun dealers as a means of raising revenue. In Washington state, police are mandated by law to sell these guns back to gun dealers. Many argue that guns are only inanimate objects and that their misuse is the result of the behavior of certain individuals who possess guns. In a nation where a handgun is manufactured every 20 seconds, and half a million guns change hands every day, we do not need to recycle criminals' guns back into public circulation. There are too many guns out there already. Surely these reclaimed weapons could be put to better use in another form. In Boston, the guns collected during the Gun Buy-Back program will be melted down and transformed into an art work, possibly with a theme of peace.

Find out what happens to confiscated guns in your own community. Don't let guns be resold and possibly get into the wrong hands again. Let local officials know that your city or town should not be in the gun trafficking business. Any revenue realized from gun resales may not be worth the risk to your community. Money from resales may have to go toward prosecuting more criminal cases if those guns end up in illegal hands and toward health care and emergency services for gunshot victims.

32 Demand Enforcement Of Existing Gun Laws.

There are approximately 25,000 gun laws in the United States—most of them are enforceable if that is made to be a priority. In the absence of a strong, uniform national gun code and policy these laws are all we have in terms of action by the criminal justice system, in regard to the illegal use and misuse of guns.

But the law is only as good as the enforcement.

For example, since 1975, Massachusetts has had the "Bartley-Fox" law which provides for a mandatory "minimum" one year prison term for those offenders convicted of carrying an unlicensed firearm. When the law was first approved, amid a swirl of publicity and extensive media coverage, gun assaults dropped dramatically in Boston. It was obvious that "the word" had gotten out to the criminal element that the state was serious about curtailing the rampant gun violence within its borders. Signs were erected at the Massachusetts Turnpike, and other entry points into Massachusetts, warning all visitors about the risks of carrying an unlicensed firearm into the state. Police were jubilant over the enactment of the law which gave them an added measure of protection in the course of their dangerous duties.

As time went by, it became apparent that the law was not working as gun violence began to rear its ugly head once again in the Bay state. Some saw a problem with the wording of the law itself. The mandatory jail term could only be meted out for an individual convicted of "carrying" an unlicensed firearm as opposed to simple "possession". Thus if a gun was found on the seat of a car, instead of on a suspect's person, the law did not apply. Also, many times the accused illegal gun-toters were allowed to plead "no contest" to the charges and thus avoid conviction and the mandatory jail time. The law does not apply to juveniles or to an unlicensed firearm found in a person's house.

Recently, the Bartley-Fox law was amended to plug up the "loophole" which made the distinction between "carrying" and "possession" moot by extending the mandatory prison provisions to possession as well as to carrying. In light of the skyrocking number of armed youth assaults and violence, many feel that the law should be amended to include juveniles.

The test of the law is, again, its enforcement which many law enforcement officials in Massachusetts say is still lacking. Few individuals are charged under the law, they maintain, in spite of the record number of individuals being arrested for crimes and violent acts involving unregistered firearms. Others say that the law severely limits leeway for a judge in considering mitigating circumstances. They say that it is applied more often to poor, inner-city residents than it is to other individuals.

In any event, the Bartley-Fox law remains largely unenforced in Massachusetts, according to a recent study by the Boston Police Department. This is unfortunate, considering its potential for giving the criminal element second thoughts about using guns in the course of their crimes. It would also be a strong deterrent to gun runners and smugglers since the one-year jail term is the "minimum" that they must serve upon conviction. Massachusetts judges have the latitude to sentence them to much longer terms under the Bartley-Fox law.

33 Cooperate With Local Police.

Not long ago, the majority of police officers opposed gun control...then the reality of the 1990s caused a great shift in their thinking. The sheer number of guns, their easy accessibility, enhanced firepower of new automatic 9mm pistols (which can penetrate a protective vest), and assault weapons have placed our police in more danger than ever before. Indeed, many police departments have replaced the standard .38 revolver with the more high tech 9mm pistol—just to keep up with the firepower of drug dealers and youth gangs.

In a country and an age when anyone can easily get a gun, every call that a police officer responds to can prove to be extremely dangerous, even "domestic disturbances". Twenty years ago these calls were routine. As the incidence of domestic violence related shootings clearly evidences, these calls cannot be taken lightly. Some police officers told me that they now wear bulletproof vests during their entire shifts—not just when participating in particularly high-risk assignments.

As the idea of "community policing" gains in popularity, where police officers are assigned to specific neighborhoods and get to know residents and merchants, the improved level of communication will provide a better working relationship between police and the community. These relationships built on trust will help to reduce crime and guns. It is comforting when everyone is working together on the front lines to take back our neighborhoods from the criminals and "gunnies".

34 Join Or Organize A Neighborhood Crime Watch.

If there is a Crime Watch group in your neighborhood, join it. Lend a hand and help to watch out for your neighbors who are watching out for you.

If there is no Crime Watch in your neighborhood, why not start one? The police need your help because you know your community. You see things. You hear things. Help your community and help yourself. With your assistance the police can prevent crime instead of having to respond to it. The police cannot do the job alone.

Why not volunteer to form or head up a special subcommittee on guns? Find out what the gun situation is in your community and then find out what can be done about it. Knowledge is power.

35 Monitor Disposition Of Gun Cases.

As a Crime Watch member or as a citizen you can go to court to monitor cases. This will give you an idea of how your local court is disposing of gun cases. Call your local newspaper reporters and tell them what you are doing. Share any relevant information with them. Inform your community through a Crime Watch newsletter and provide information at community meetings. Even judges who are appointed for life are still subject to public scrutiny. They are sensitive to how their actions are viewed by the community and the press.

For help in organizing a local crime watch, contact your local police department, other Crime Watch groups in your city or town, or write:

Crime Prevention Council
("Getting Together")
1700 K Street, NW
Washington, DC 20006

36 Suggest The Creation Of A Special Gun Squad For Your Local Police Department.

Many police departments are understaffed and stretched to their limits. Hopefully, under President Clinton's crime package a massive infusion of federal funds will help local police departments to restore staffing levels. Funds are earmarked for the hiring of an additional 200,000 police officers across the nation. Every police department should have a special "gun squad", working in shifts around the clock to attack the glut of illegal guns in our communities.

Working in close cooperation with federal, state and local agencies, the gun squads could conduct "sting"–like operations, similar to drug busts. They could aggressively investigate, apprehend and prosecute people who are dealing in illegal guns.

We need a change in our thinking, strategy and procedure. Guns should become the priority and drugs should be a secondary objective. The "war on drugs" should NOT be abandoned, but illegal guns are killing far more people than illegal drugs. The life and safety of citizens should be our top priority. Guns are easier to locate and detect than drugs; and guns are the "muscle" of the illegal drug business. What is a drug dealer without a gun?

37 Suggest The Creation Of A Special Gun Court.

If your city or town does not have a court that deals strictly with gun-related crime, suggest that one be created. Or, at least, suggest that a special session of your local court be added for gun violence and crime.

Since there are so many gun laws and potential "loopholes", it makes sense to have a court that deals solely with guns. This court can work with the special police gun squad and prosecutors trained and experienced in gun law and cases.

38 Show Support For Gun Victims In Your Community.

Too often we turn our heads away from violence as we feel grateful that it did not happen to us. That's human nature. But we cannot continue to shrug off our neighbor's pain and misery as "none of my business". Nor can we continue to distance ourselves from their plight by blaming the victim or assume that a gunshot victim was shot while engaged in unlawful activities. These attitudes only weaken our communities and impede the fight to get guns out of our neighborhoods.

Gunshots affect many more people than just the victim. Entire families and even neighborhoods can be traumatized by a shooting. There are so many shooting victims today that even the mass media cannot show all of the grief and misery that lingers long after a victim is buried. Guilt, anguish, remorse and bitterness often leads survivors to alcoholism, divorce and even suicide.

Don't shun a member of the community who has been a victim of a shooting or one who has lost a relative or loved one to gun violence. Show some support. Offer your help, especially when the victim is a young person. Can you imagine how painful it is for a grief-stricken mother to receive a bill for ambulance services long after her son is dead? Often she has had to beg and borrow just to raise money to bury him.

True charity looks at the need and not the cause. No one deserves to die at thirteen.

If we cannot acknowledge the grief and pain of a neighbor, then we cannot confront the reality of what guns are doing to our community. We can't hide from what is happening out there in our streets. Like it or not, we are all in this together.

39 Find Out How Many Licensed Gun Dealers There Are In Your City Or Town.

As noted, there are nearly 300,000 licensed gun dealers in the U.S. There are more gun dealers than gas stations. Getting a federal license to deal in guns is easier than getting a driver's license in many states. An applicant simply fills out a form and pays a small fee, about $30—and they must not be a convicted felon. One must attest to his or her own mental health. The law does not required that one demonstrate proficiency with firearms. If a background check is conducted, it is cursory at best because there are only about 400 Federal Alcohol, Tobacco and Firearms Bureau agents (ATF). These agents monitor all of the gun dealers in America, as well as perform many other duties.

In 1990, out of the 34,000 applications for a firearms dealers' license, only 75 were turned down.

Most licensed gun dealers, perhaps 80 per cent, do not have a regular business but operate out of their homes. Thus a licensed gun dealer could be your next door neighbor who deals in bulk shipments of thousands of guns, without your knowledge.

In 1993, a federally licensed gun dealer in the Boston area was indicted, along with some others, for illegally filing off the serial numbers of hundreds of handguns and selling them, reportedly, to youth gangs. The guns that the police were able to trace had been sold in Boston's inner city in 1990 and 1991, two of the bloodiest years in the city's history.

More public school students were shot to death in that period than at any time in Boston's history.

President Clinton's crime package calls for strengthening regulation of gun dealers. The ATF is now tracing guns used by young people in crimes without being asked to do so by local authorities. Both of these initiatives will help. In the meantime, we need to take more responsibility on the local level to insure that gun sales are strictly above board.

The special local police department Gun Squad could serve that purpose.

40 Demand Closer Supervision And Monitoring Of Gun Dealers In Your City, Town Or Community.

With hundreds of thousands of licensed gun dealers operating primarily out of their homes, and thousands more receiving licenses to deal in an array of firearms, a closer look should be taken at record-keeping and security by local authorities. (For only $30,000 a license can import mortars and bazookas.)

There is a myth that illegal guns flowing into a given community all come from "out of state", brought in by bus or train from another state where gun laws are lenient. There is no doubt that this is true in some cases, but not always.

In 1993, the local Boston branch of the ATF conducted a study tracking 1,258 firearms that had been recovered by Boston Police between October 1989 and June 1992. The ATF found that although 61 percent of the guns came from outside of Massachusetts, including 46 other states and some foreign countries, **Massachusetts itself was the single sole source for the guns that had been used in criminal activity, accounting for 39 percent of the 1,258 pistols, revolvers and shotguns seized by police.** The majority of the cheaper guns were recovered in Boston Police District Area B, a predominantly inner city sector.

The special agent in charge of the Boston ATF bureau stated that similar ATF studies have shown the "home state" to be the major provider of firearms that end up being used in crimes. He added that, **"Many of the guns had been obtained legally and resold to criminals."**

41 Demand Liability Laws For Gun Deaths And Injuries.

Guns kill about 65 people every day in the United States—approximately the same as the number killed by drunk drivers each day in our country. Yet few states have enacted strong laws to allow compensation for victims of guns that end up in the wrong hands.

Gun manufacturers and dealers should be held legally responsible and morally accountable for the death and maiming of citizens. Two hundred thousand people are injured by firearms in our country each year. There is a tendency to "blame the victim" in gunshot cases but, increasingly, the victim is an average, law-abiding, hard-working citizen caught in an epidemic of gun violence. Such a shooting occurred on the New York commuter train in December 1993. A deranged individual opened fire on a crowded train at rush hour, killing five people and wounding many others with a 9mm automatic pistol. The gun had been purchased legally in California. This incident drew national attention. However, many similar cases in which people are shot and wounded while simply minding their own business are on record and continue to rise. In 1985, four innocent bystanders were shot to death in New York City. By 1990, the number had risen to forty.

Health and medical care costs for gunshot victims in America exceeds $14 billion each year. (Estimate of total gun violence, including crime, accidents and suicides is $135 billion, according to National Public Services Research Institute. *USA Today*, 12/29/93.)

Forty million Americans, including ten million

children, have no health insurance. Many of these uninsured citizens are among the growing list of gunshot victims.

Gun manufacturers and dealers must be made to take responsibility for the damage that their wares are doing to our citizenry, just as automobile manufacturers and dealers and the tobacco industry have been made liable for negative effects of their products. Today the attitude of the gun manufacturers and dealers is that their responsibility ends after guns cross the counters, even when their guns are purchased by "strawmen" (to be given or sold to someone who should not and cannot legally possess a gun). Gun dealers and manufacturers don't even take responsibility when guns are sold to mentally unstable persons, or when guns are stolen from the factory or the dealer, or when they are pilfered in large quantities during shipment.

State legislators have the power to enact "wrongful death" statutes. This would be the starting place for action in your community.

42 Initiate Legal Action.

In the absence of tough liability laws in many states, victims of gun violence are going to court in increasing numbers to seek damages when they believe that gun dealers have been negligent.

In the Spring of 1993, the California Court of Appeals found that a gun sale to a "strawman" (who later gave the gun to a minor) was illegal and that the gun dealer (who allegedly encouraged the sale) could be forced to pay damages to the family of a man who was fatally shot by the gun. The 19 year old who was convicted in the shooting death of a man at a party had visited the gun shop. He was turned down while attempting to buy a 9mm semiautomatic pistol because he was not 21. He asked if his grandmother could buy it for him. The clerk replied that he could sell the gun to her if she were a qualified buyer but not "...just so she could give the gun to him." The minor returned to the store with his grandmother where she purchased the 9mm Smith and Wesson, which he had been admiring in his earlier visits. Twelve days later, as the gun was being handled at a beer drinking party, the teenager shot and killed his friend.

In "very strong language", according to the Center to Prevent Handgun Violence (*Legal Action Report*, May 1993), the judge who was writing for the court ruled that "[The gun dealer's] construction of the law would nullify [the gun law], give our imprimatur to a 'strawman' sale, and immunize firearms dealers who circumvent the letter and spirit of the firearm control laws." When the case goes before a jury, the jury will decide whether or not there was "conscious knowledge" on the part of the gun dealer that the grandmother was, in fact, acting as a "straw" or intermediary to purchase the gun for her teenage grandson.

Another potential liability case, from 1991, involves the sale of a gun to a former mental patient in Virginia, a state known for its lax gun laws. (Virginia recently passed a law which prevents an individual from buying more than twelve handguns per month. Previously, many people were coming in from other states to buy guns. Reportedly, thirty-five percent of all handguns found in crime scenes in New York City originate in Virginia.) The former mental patient bought the gun from a store called "Guns Unlimited". He was allowed to buy the handgun, even though he refused to sign the federal form required for such a purchase. Ten day later, he used the gun to shoot an insurance executive on a crowded street in Philadelphia.

In January 1992, the same store was ordered to pay $105,000 in damages by a Virginia Beach jury for selling a semiautomatic assault pistol to a 15 year old. The boy's 37 year old cousin had acted as a "straw" to buy the gun. Two months after receiving the gun, he shot and killed a high school teacher. (See the "Story of a Gun" by Eric Larson. *Atlantic*, January 1992.) This is considered a landmark precedent-setting case.

These two cases illustrate both the dangers of indiscriminate gun sales and the increasing willingness of the courts to assess responsibility and liability of gun dealers for the death of victims of their wares. The suits were aided by the Legal Action Project of the Center to Prevent Handgun Violence, which offers an "Outline of Gun Manufacturer and Seller Liability Issues". It is available to attorneys, free of charge, to assist in the preparation of law suits against negligent gun dealers. Write: **Center to Prevent Handgun Violence** (Attention: Legal Defense Project), 1225 Eye Street, NW, Suite 1100, Washington, DC 20005.

In their newsletter, the Legal Defense Project notes that the U.S. Consumer Product Safety Commission is developing safety standards for child-resistant disposable cigarette lighters, as they have done for thousands of other products. Yet firearms are specifically "excluded" from regulation by that agency.

Perhaps what is needed is a class-action suit by thousands of American gun victims against the gun manufacturers and dealers where negligence is suspected. (Ten gun manufacturers make five billion rounds of ammunition per year.) The idea of a class-action suit was proposed to me by my friend, Jim Keeney, 82 years young, of Sturbridge, Massachusetts. A newspaper writer who frequently writes about gun issues and an avid Red Sox fan (which demonstrates his persistence), Jim believes that a multimillion dollar nationwide class-action suit will force manufacturers and dealers to finally begin to accept responsibility for the damage and carnage caused by their products. He also believes that if manufacturers and dealers stand to lose some of their billions of dollars in profits, they will be more inclined to tighten up procedures and more motivated to police themselves. I agree with Jim. What do you think?

Note: Recently the Wal-Mart retail chain (America's largest) announced that it would remove handguns from the 700 of its 2,000 stores that sell them. Other retail and sporting goods stores have already "gone out of the gun business, forever" such as MVP Sports, a major retail chain in New England. Apparently, store owners and managers are recognizing potential legal problems and financial losses from selling guns. They also see a potential loss of customers. Some parents are uncomfortable bringing their children in buy ice skates or baseball equipment and being confronted by an array of handguns on display.

43 Examine Your Local Gun Laws. Ask Questions.

Traditionally, laws regulating firearms have been slow to pass. Don't assume that everything that needs to be done has been done. Equally important, don't assume what has been done has not been "undone".

For example, recently, it came to light that in Massachusetts (known for its "tough" gun laws), it is not a felony for an individual to illegally sell a gun to another person, even a minor. It is presently a misdemeanor, punishable by a $500 fine for a first offense. Since the courts are clogged with felony cases these offenders are rarely even brought to trial. Legislation has been filed to upgrade the penalty for this offense. In the meantime, some individuals have been able to turn a quick profit in a sluggish economy by illegally selling guns that they purchased legally.

No one knows how many people have been murdered, raped and robbed by criminals armed with these guns. But it is safe to assume that these guns were not purchased for target shooting.

44 Beware Of Deadly Loopholes In Your Local Gun Laws.

Gun laws, like many other laws, can be confusing and they are often amended to allow exceptions. This can prove fatal.

For example, in December of 1992, in Great Barrington, Massachusetts, an 18 year old college student bought a military style semiautomatic assault weapon. He purchased the rifle merely by showing a driver's license and he ordered ammunition through the mail. He went on a shooting spree, killing two people and wounding two others. Being an out-of-state resident, he was allowed to legally purchase the rifle without a permit. The intent of the "loophole" was to allow out-of-state hunters to be able to purchase a hunting weapon. Ironically, and tragically in this case, the original law provided for no such exemptions but was quietly amended after it's enactment.

Gun laws are designed to protect the public. Be sure that your state and local laws are applied uniformly. Be vigilant for any proposed changes in your local firearms code that may appear innocuous on the surface yet may prove to have deadly consequences.

45 Organize On A Local, Grassroots Level.

It took more than six years and more than 100,000 handgun deaths for Congress to approve the "Brady Bill", a relatively mild measure that mandates a waiting period before an individual may purchase a handgun. With this in mind, find ways that you can keep the momentum going for sane and reasonable legislation "from the ground up"—from you, the People.

As gun violence continues to engulf our society, the need for Americans to be involved in this issue is greater than ever.

Don't be put off or intimidated because you may not be an "expert" on guns or gun laws. The fact that you live in this country qualifies you as an expert on gun violence because so many of us have been touched by it both directly and indirectly.

Consider this: if federally-licensed gun dealers are not required to demonstrate proficiency with firearms or even to know the difference between a revolver and a shotgun, then why should you?

The issue of gun violence has become a universal one in American communities. It is no longer "liberal vs. conservative" or Republican vs. Democrat. It crosses all lines—racial, generational, gender, class and political.

The movement to free us from the fear of guns and curtail the crime and violence (that unrestricted access to firearms fosters) is building and growing across America.

In Washington State, a group known as "Washington CeaseFire" (formerly Washington Citizens for Rational Handgun Control) is organizing on a grassroots level. The group will address gun violence in their state, which had more handgun deaths in 1992 than all of Canada and Great Britain combined.

Washington CeaseFire is one of many groups across the nation working to prevent gun violence by educating and informing citizens on a community level and by supporting violence prevention programs. Their legislative agenda includes the repealing of a law that was sponsored by the National Rifle Association which requires local law enforcement authorities to resell weapons seized by police to gun dealers.

Every community is different; gun problems and laws may vary in every locality. Organizing on the local level is the first step in gathering and sharing information that citizens need to make rational decisions about what they would like to see done legislatively.

Talk to friends, neighbors, teachers, police, public health professionals and others in your community. Form a "CeaseFire" type group in your own community and go from there. Remember, anything you do to help stop gun violence is probably more than is being done now. Doing "something" is preferable to doing nothing. Write to the CeaseFire group in Washington state for their support:

Washington CeaseFire
P. O. Box 15644
Seattle, WA 98115-0644

46 Write Letters To The Editor And To Elected Officials.

The term "silent majority" has never been more applicable than for today's citizens who have had enough of gun violence but don't know what to do about it.

Dashing off a letter to a newspaper or magazine editor is a good way of letting off steam while doing something productive. Also let your elected officials and your fellow citizens know how you feel. You may be surprised to learn how many people feel as fed up with violence as you do.

It isn't necessary to take sides in terms of being "pro"- or "anti"-gun. However, it is important to keep the issue of gun violence alive and to demand action by those in power. Your taxes support your politicians; therefore, they should help to make your community safe. Tell them what is important to you. For example, you want to be safe walking down the street. And you want your children to be safe at school.

Writing to elected officials is also important. This enables you to be on record, even if you feel that you're not being heard or if you only receive a form letter in response to your call for action. If you are not satisfied with a response from your officials, write again or call to ask for a meeting. Remember, the elected officials work for *you.* Don't let them off the hook because there's too much at stake.

47 Attend Public Hearings.

Many times legislation concerning firearms is decided at public hearings. Traditionally, those who do not favor stronger measures to restrict access and availability of guns tend to far outnumber those who do favor more control. There are many reasons for this. Still, it is important for those who want to see more restrictions to attend these hearings and to express their opinions. This is not always easy, especially when you feel outnumbered and may be subjected to unpleasant responses from those who disagree with you. But keep in mind that the democratic process is not anyone's private domain. It belongs to you as much as to anyone. You have an absolute right to appear, to give testimony and to be heard. The climate is much better today for those who feel that guns and gun violence are out of control. Unquestionably, these people outnumber those who feel that there should be no restrictions of any kind.

Hemingway once described courage as "grace under pressure". You may feel a great deal of pressure should you choose to testify at a public hearing on guns. But your courage in speaking out will give heart to others who are also fed up with gun violence in our society. Your actions will show your elected officials that you care about your community and it will motivate them to care.

Stand up and be counted. It's your right, your community, and your country.

48 Organize A Referendum On Guns In Your Community.

One of the best ways for citizens to send a message to their elected officials is through an advisory question or a non-binding referendum. The "non-binding" approach has many benefits, as opposed to citizens trying to pass a particular law on guns through a binding question.

Most citizens are not lawyers or experts on gun laws. If a question is not worded properly, it could be taken apart in court on a "technicality". Since the question is not binding, there are no grounds for it to be attacked by an opposing group or pro-gun interest because a non-binding question is not threatening. It merely asks voters' opinions about a particular issue.

Another advantage to a purely advisory ballot question is that it is an official means of surveying attitudes and documenting the will of the people. They can give their opinion in the privacy and sanctity of the voting booth, without fear of harassment or intimidation by those who may not agree with them. It is a way to send a clear message to those in power. Even though it is "symbolic", an advisory opinion from the voters can influence public policy. The results may even surprise some observers and elected officials.

Such was a case in November 1992 in Boston when a question was placed on the ballot asking voters' opinion of a ban on handguns in the city. The question was placed on the ballot by a signature drive organized by a group of inner-city residents who called themselves...

CEASEFIRE, Boston ("Citizens to Ensure A Safe Environment-Firearms Reduction Effort").

The question read, simply:

"Shall the (state) representative from this district be instructed to vote in favor of legislation banning the sale, possession and transfer of handguns in the City of Boston?"

It is important to note that CeaseFire, Boston held no fund-raisers. We donated money out of our own pockets to pay for a few stamps, stationery, a $10 a month mail service and buttons that we had made to wear during the signature drive. We tried to get the question on the ballot in as many Boston neighborhoods as possible, within the deadline given to us by state law.

After some initial publicity when we began the signature drive, interest from the major newspapers began to wane. There had been no interest or coverage from the major Boston television stations.

We concentrated our outreach and educational efforts on appearances before community groups, neighborhood events and social activities. We sent letters and press releases to the weekly newspapers in Boston's diverse neighborhoods. Our outreach effort was aimed toward letting people know that the question (known as "Question 5") would be appearing in this book, *50 Things You Can Do About Guns.*

We did not use sensationalism, even though shootings were occurring almost daily in the city. We told people the truth about the referendum, explaining what it could do and could not do. We informed them that it would not become law if approved but that it could help to send a message to the "powers that be" in Boston. It would let politicians know that we wanted more done to control gun violence.

We did not try to "sway" people into voting to ban handguns but we advised them that the question would be on the ballot. And we reminded people to vote, regardless of how they intended to vote on the issue.

In spite of an effort to defeat Question 5 (in the form of paid advertising and leafleting by a local gun advocacy group), it carried overwhelmingly when Bostonians went to the polls in November 1992. The people voted to ban handguns by a 3-2 margin. Sixty-two per cent of Bostonians who cast a vote on Question 5 voted "Yes" to a ban. Question 5 carried in 81 out of 102 precincts in which it appeared on the ballot. It was approved in "liberal" wards as well as in traditionally conservative blue-collar districts.

Although the vote was non-binding, it served many positive purposes.

Most voters felt empowered by being able to vote on the issue of handguns in their city. Even though the referendum would not become law, the voters felt that at least they could be heard. They felt that they were "doing something", by pulling levers in the voting booths, the prime symbol of our democratic system.

The referendum also produced some tangible results. In the fall of 1993, an ordinance was introduced into the Boston City Council that would prohibit the sale or possession of a handgun by a minor. The sponsor of the ordinance used the results of the referendum as evidence of clear public support for the measure. The Mayor approved and signed the measure and sent it to the state legislature for final approval under Boston's "Home Rule" provisions.

Also, in the fall of 1993, the two finalists in the contest for Mayor adopted the position of banning handguns in Boston, in accordance with the wishes of the voters. Such a position would have been considered "political suicide" just a year before. It was a position that they would have been unlikely to take had it not been for the message sent by the people through the referendum. "Surveys" are one thing, votes are another.

The voters' message was a powerful one and one that was obviously heard.

Following the referendum, candidates for City Council in Boston assumed much stronger positions on handguns than ever before—even candidates who hailed from traditionally conservative districts. The candidates deserve credit for taking stronger, more nontraditional stands on handguns. But it was the people, the citizens of Boston, who led the way.

A similar political course of action can be taken in your own community. Even if your non-binding referendum on guns (however you choose to word it) fails to "pass", it will generate interest among the electorate. It will help to keep the gun issue in the forefront, provide a forum for meaningful and intelligent discussion, and promote ideas about what people can do to help.

If you choose to place an advisory question on the ballot, no matter what the results, think of it as a beginning (and not an end) to your activism on the gun violence issue.

As Abraham Lincoln advised, "just keep whittling away".

49 Organize A Gun Buy-Back Program In Your Community.

Many communities, particularly major urban areas hit hard by soaring gun violence and crime, have initiated programs to allow individuals to turn in guns anonymously and receive a modest "bounty" (such as a $50.00 money order). These gun "buy-back" programs vary in structure and have met with varying degrees of success. Even skeptics agree that "doing something is better than doing nothing". If a buy-back program saves just one life, it is well worth it.

Most programs rely upon private donations and public support. A close working relationship with the local police department and law enforcement authorities is the key to a successful buy-back program.

Since 80% of gun victims know their attackers, the merits of a program allowing citizens to dispose of unwanted guns are obvious. The absence of a gun reduces the likelihood of murder by gun as a result of domestic violence or family dispute. It greatly reduces the possibility of suicide and accidental shootings.

Few citizens know how to lawfully dispose of a gun. A buy-back program, sanctioned and supervised by local authorities (and promising anonymity to those turning in guns), makes it easier for people to get rid of their unwanted weapons. A small "bounty" helps to cover some of the initial expense of a gun.

People in St. Louis, Missouri were reported to have collected more than 7,000 guns. After their gun buy-back efforts, there was a 2/3 drop in that city's homicide rate.

In the summer of 1993, the Massachusetts Citizens for Safety organized a gun buy-back program in Boston. More than 1,000 guns were collected before the privately raised funds were depleted.

The Massachusetts group combined their gun buy-back program with youth violence prevention programs, sports and recreational programs such as a "Soccer Marathon for Peace". These groups also helped to raise funds for their many activities. Their gun buy-back program was well-organized and received the support and cooperation of the police department and other law enforcement agencies. The media was generally supportive. The program received full support of a Boston daily newspaper, which helped greatly by informing the public of the purpose and potential benefits of the buy-back. Local advertising agencies and television stations provided public service message. Ads also appeared on subway trains and buses.

The core of the Boston Gun Buy-Back program was the network of grassroots community organizations, agencies and groups developed by the Citizens for Safety over a period of years. These efforts provided solid communication with neighborhood residents and established trust and credibility for the program. For information and support, contact:

Massachusetts Citizens for Safety
100 Massachusetts Avenue
Boston, MA 02115
(617) 266-2171

Note: About 45 American cities now have gun buy-back programs. Some are sponsored by the city or town, others are sponsored by private groups, and some are a partnership between local government and community groups. The program in New York City, which has about one million (mostly illegal) guns, was enhanced by the support of Toys R US during the holiday season of 1993. Guns could be exchanged for $100 gift certificates. The New York City program was such a phenomenal success that it may be expanded coast to coast.

50 Look Beyond The Brady Bill.

Jim and Sarah Brady deserve high praise for their untiring efforts and years of hard work to secure passage of the "Brady Bill". This bill was named for Jim Brady who was shot by a deranged gunman along with former President Ronald Reagan in 1981.

The Brady Bill, signed into law by President Clinton, is now the law of the land. It provides for a nationally mandated waiting period before an individual may purchase a handgun, a "cooling off" period so to speak, which will help to save lives.

The Brady law also represents the first federal firearms control legislation since the 1968 Federal Firearms Control Act, passed following the assassination of Robert Kennedy. Unfortunately, that law only prohibited the importation of "Saturday Night Specials", cheap and flimsy handguns from other countries. They still could be manufactured, and still are being manufactured, here at home.

Finally, we "are" making progress in moving toward a safe and sane national gun policy. The Bradys and President Clinton have indicated that they will continue to press for stronger measures to curb the unrestricted access to firearms, which holds all of us hostage to fear.

While we pursue the dream of a rational national gun policy, we should keep in mind that there is still much that we can do on the local level as individuals and as groups concerned about violence in our community. This is the purpose of this book, *50 Things You Can Do About Guns.*

The Brady Bill was just a beginning in the long, hard road ahead. But we can continue working together toward our goals of stopping gun violence.

As John Kennedy once observed, "Everyone can make a difference, and each of us must try."

In the words of Martin Luther King Jr., "There is a time to let things happen and a time to make them happen."

We have let things happen long enough. It's time to make things happen.

Good luck with your community efforts.

Epilogue

"An alternative to the use of guns
    can be the use of words
    rather than bullets.
  Time, prayer and hope
    rather than the taking of other lives."

Pat Engel
(writer, artist, concerned citizen)
San Francisco, CA
April 1994

ADDENDA

Jamaica Plain Citizen

Roxbury Citizen

The Outstanding Civic Asset Of A Community Is The Integrity Of Its Newspaper

Page 14, January 7, 1993

Cease-Fire Leader Urges Boycott of Sporting Goods Chain

The founder of a Boston group which successfully placed a non-binding referendum on the question of a handgun ban for the city recently called for a boycott of MVP Sports to protest the local sporting goods chain's "irresponsibility" in both its advertising and its method of unloading its stock of guns — particularly its handguns.

The company has announced a "going out of the gun business forever" after forty years in the gun business.

James M. Murray of Jamaica Plain, founder of the group CEASE-FIRE (Citizens to Ensure A Safe Environment-Firearms Reduction Effort) referring to a large display ad for the sale which has been running in a major Boston newspaper off and on since the first week in December, called for a boycott of the sale and the MVP Sports stores in Danvers, Brockton, Norwood, Woburn, and Nashua where the gun sale is running.

Murray charged that the ads are "in bad taste at best given the current situation with domestic violence and street crime in our society. At worst, they are a shameless exploitation of the fears that this same violence has heightened in the name of quick and easy profits and economic expediency."

The ads, said Murray encourage the public to take advantage of savings up to 70 percent on handguns "new and used" and, in excitable language, urges consumers to hurry to the stores and "get 'em while they last."

"In a time when we are still feeling the glow of celebrating the hope and the message of Peace on Earth, it is disheartening to see such a cynical attitude of profits before people by the dumping of handguns, which are made only to kill human beings, on the public."

Murray noted that last summer many major retail outlets were urged to remove high powered squirt guns from their shelves following sporadic incidents involving their misuse. "We know the potential for misuse of real guns," Murray said. "Should we not expect the same sense of civic responsibility from gun dealers as we do from toy companies?"

Murray added that he had written to the President of MVP Sports when he first saw the ads in mid-December. "I suggested that MVP Sports could generate invaluable goodwill by publicly having their surplus handguns melted down to be used to make ice skates or sporting equipment for kids in lieu of any short-term economic gain from selling the guns. I never heard from anyone in the company, but I have heard from other parents who are upset with the ads and the sale."

Murray urged the 60 percent of Boston voters who voted to ban handguns in the City to boycott MVP Sports until the company agreed to show more corporate and civic responsibility.

"A boycott is a legitimate means of social protest." Murray said. "MVP Sports has a right to advertise and to sell their wares, but we have a right, as consumers, as citizens and concerned parents, to protest their actions."

Some good can come out of any situation." Murray concluded. "The MVP Sports sale points out the glut of handguns on the market today and raises the question as to why we are still manufacturing handguns in this country at the rate of one every twenty seconds if we cannot sell the ones we have without drastic markdowns and frenzied sales and advertising."

CEASE-FIRE *Citizens To Ensure A Safe Environment*

BOSTON *Firearms Reduction Effort*

Jamaica Plain, MA 02130

BOSTON SUNDAY HERALD, JUNE 14, 1992 **7**

Flynn seeks non-binding vote on handgun ban

By LAURA BROWN

Less than a week after calling on storeowners to stop selling high-powered water guns, Mayor Raymond L. Flynn expanded his message by backing a non-binding ballot question seeking opinions on a citywide handgun ban.

Organizers of the referendum drive have collected enough signatures to get the question on the ballot in Charlestown and are working on a similar effort in other parts of the city.

Flynn described the drive as a "powerful" way to make people talk about guns and violence.

"This gives people another opportunity through a legitimate process — democracy at the ballot box — to express their point of view to their congressional leaders," Flynn said during a recent interview.

"You need national fire-

'urn to Page 19

Flynn wants voters' opinion on gun ban

From Page 7

arms legislation, because you can't do it alone at the local level," he added.

Flynn has backed a national ban on assault weapons — which he claimed the controversial "Super Soaker" water-guns imitate — and a waiting period for the purchase of handguns.

He said the ballot drive "couldn't come at a more appropriate time" than the middle of a presidential campaign.

"Because there's a presidential election (voters) have got to decide, they've got to **talk** about violence, particularly as it relates to young

people," Flynn said.

"This is at an epidemic proportion in America," he added. "In cities all across our country, young people (are) brought up feeling a glorification of guns and violence."

The group that launched the referendum drive calls itself CEASE-FIRE, or Citizens to Ensure A Safe Environment — Firearms Reduction Effort, and was organized by former City Council candidates and Vietnam veterans James Murray and Boyce Slayman.

Murray said the group "welcomed and appreciated" the mayor's support. □

Jamaica Plain/Roxbury Citizen   12/31/92

Letter to the Editor

Crisis Cries Out for Gun Control

To the Editor:

The outrage that took place recently in Brighton, which saw yet another innocent life tragically and violently snuffed out by a killer with a handgun, proves that the system can no longer protect its citizens—especially women and children who are increasingly the target of such attacks and are most vulnerable.

In the meantime, the sale, transfe, production and importation of handguns continues unchecked, with a handgun manufactured every 20 seconds, thus adding two million more each year. Add these to the 200 million or so in our nation's stockpile and factor in military weapons and we can deduce that there are more guns than people in the United States. And the guns and the casualties continue to mount, with about 30,000 dead and 200,000 wounded each year in the U.S.

Given that the criminal justice system and related protective services and restraining orders have proven totally ineffective in protecting its citizens, it should be readily apparent that the only way to protect ourselves, women and children in particular, is to get rid of the guns, especially the handguns. (More than 70 percent of handgun victims know or are related to their assailants.)

Back in 1974, a poll conducted by Congressman Joseph Moakley indicated that 68 percent of the people supported limiting the sale and possession of handguns to the police as a means of reducing street crime.

This past November, more than 60 percent of the Bostonians voted on a non-binding referendum to ban the sale, tranfer and possession of handguns to the police as a means of reducing street crime.

This past November, more than 60 percent of the Bostonians voted on a non-binding referendum to ban the sale, transfer and possession of handguns in the City of Boston. People are fed up with guns and gun violence, and want something done.

Clearly, we need more than "stopgap" measures and "plugging up loopholes" in existing laws that may only be "unplugged" quietly at a later time at the urging of the gun lobby, which represents the gun manufacturers and the 241,000 gun dealers in the U.S. who are permitted to sell their wares with only a $30 license and a routine, cursory background check.

Easily more than 100,000 Americans have been murdered by handguns and more than a million wounded since that 1974 survey was conducted.

In Boston, we have witnessed many tragic and horrifying shootings - recently one in broad daylight while a bus full of school children looked on in fear.

The situation cries out for action, for we are in the grip of a genuine emergency, a national crisis of violence of epidemic proportions that threatens the very existence of our society.

It is time to end the sale, manufacture and importation—immediately—of handguns, and use the latitude given us by the United States Supreme Court and many other federal courts, such as the Seventh Circuit Court, which upheld a ban on the private possession of handguns in Morton Grove, Illinois, to restore sanity to our city and our society. Because, in addition to feeding domestic violence, we are actually arming the criminals by allowing the handgun industry's juggernaut, fueled by greed and profits and shielded by the powerful gun lobby from any attempts to rein it in, to tear its way through our society leaving thousands of dead in its wake each year.

At the very least, the City Council should hold public hearings to establish the truth about handguns and where they are coming from. We may find, like it says in the song by Crosby, Stills and Nash, "...someting going on that surely won't stand the light of day."

The people have spoken. They need to be heard.

Jim Murray

Bostonians can vote on gun control

Another Boston teen was shot to death and yet some people are still opposed to gun control on a national level ("13-year-old shot to death on Blue Hill Ave." Oct. 18).

This nightmare of handgun violence continues. And we need to wake up.

A non-binding question will appear on the Nov. 3 ballot in Charlestown, East Boston, South Boston, Roxbury, West Roxbury, Jamaica Plain and Mission Hill. The question seeks voters' opinion on a ban on handguns in the city of Boston.

It will *not* become law if approved, but it will keep attention focused on the issue of handgun violence and raise some questions.

Why is it that there are so many illegal guns? Where are they coming from? How is it that we can disarm entire countries abroad, but can't seem to take the guns away from our children at home?

Bostonians from all neighborhoods and backgrounds need to unite and demand answers to these questions. We don't want our children growing up in the armed camp that America is fast becoming.

Jim Murray,
Jamaica Plain

Boston Herald, Sunday, October 25, 1992

Send A Message —
Vote 'Yes' On Question 5

Dear Editor:

The first week of October 1992 may very well go down in history as the time when Congress — anxious to hit the campaign trail — cleared its legislative calendar and fled Washington with a frenzy and abandonment not seen since the British forces of Admiral Cockburn sacked and burned our nation's capital in 1814.

Unfortunately for America, there was no Dolly Madison on hand to rescue the serious legislation that was left behind (as she did with George Washington's portrait) such as the Brady Bill, a mild effort aimed at addressing the ugly epidemic of handgun violence in our country through a reasonable five-day waiting period before an individual may purchase a handgun.

Also in the newspapers that same weekend, Oct. 3 and 4, were the following reports:

• A Danvers man shot and killed his estranged wife, then himself.

• An 86-year-old Springfield man shot and killed a man and a woman. (He has been on probation in connection with another shooting death five years earlier.)

• A 17-year-old high school student in Maine was charged with the shooting deaths of his mother and brother.

• Four people were shot to death in a 24-hour period on the streets of Boston.

• A Hyde park man was shot to death in a parking lot in Dedham.

• In Springfield, it was discovered that the firearms card of a man who shot and killed three people, including a young boy and a pregnant woman, has never been revoked in spite of a felony conviction.

• In Florida, a candidate for state representatives was arrested in connection with the shooting of his opponent's wife. ("We believe he wanted to win the the worst way," said the local sheriff.)

• In St. Louis, a 39-year-old housewife, arguing with her '?-year-old son over his switching of television stations

threatened to shoot the T.V. but turned and shot him, instead.

• It was reported that one million women are abused in the U.S. each year.

• In Massachusetts, the number of women and children killed is now up to one every five days in spite of restraining orders which saw 700 violations out of 2000 orders issued in the past month.

There's more, but why go on. Clearly things are out of control. People are being shot at an alarming rate. And not just by the criminals, but by law-abiding citizens as well.

No amount of counseling, electronic leashes and computerized registries are going to make a dent in gun deaths and injuries unless we limit their access and availability, especially handguns, which are being manufactured at the rate of one every 20 seconds in the U.S.

There are hundreds of millions of guns in this country and millions are added every year. How many is enough?

It's readily apparent that we can't look to Washington for help, so we'd better begin to work seriously on the state and local level.

In the words of Abraham Lincoln, himself a victim of a handgun: "The job of government is to do for the people what the people cannot do for themselves." If he were alive today, he might alter it to: "The job of the people is to do what government will not do for them."

On Tuesday, Nov. 3, the voters in a cross-section of Boston's neighborhoods will be asked their opinion in a nonbinding referendum as to a ban on handguns in the city of Boston.

Question Five, which will appear on the ballot in Charlestown, will not become law if approved by the voters. But it will send a message that the people in power need to hear loudly and clearly and it could be a small but important step toward decreasing violence in a society that has declared open season upon its own women and children.

Jim Murray
CEASE-FIRE Boston

* This advisory question was certified to appear on the ballot in Charlestown, East Boston, South Boston, Roxbury, West Roxbury, Jamaica Plain, and Mission Hill.

CEASE-FIRE *Citizens to Ensure A Safe Environment Firearms Reduction Effort*

B o s t o n

May 21, 1992

.·. Jamaica Plain, MA 02130

Mayor Raymond Flynn
City Hall
Boston, MA 02201

Dear Mayor Flynn:

CEASE-FIRE Boston, in response to the horrific and wanton destruction of life that has been and is occurring in our city, is attempting to put an advisory question on the ballot re the issuance of licenses for, and the sale and ownership of handguns. We enlist your support and help.

We are not naives who think that the acceptance of such a motion by the legislature will result in a massive and immediate change in behavior, but we do think that a number of such moves nationwide, supported by the people, will clearly have positive results. Time and again the people have responded favorably to gun control issues in the United States. Time and again the Congress and other elected officials have turned their back on the people regarding this issue. They are fearful for their jobs because of the lobbying and financial largesse of the gun lobby. The legislature may be out of step with the people, as well, but you have historically not been. Your espousal of the aims of CEASE-FIRE Boston, can only be a plus for both the people and yourself as the most important urban leader in this country.

The Christian, Jewish, and Muslim communities in Boston can and will support this movement. The people most at risk - black and Hispanic - are represented in this committee as founding members. This is a people movement. The people are frightened and concerned for the future of their children, themselves, and their city. A strong statement from the people of the city on the ballot in the fall will be important. It can become a model for other such efforts in other cities, and will become a consciousness-raising tool for stronger laws regarding handgun use on a national level. But to begin we must begin. We would like to have you as a part of this movement. The desired results can be achieved, and the benefits will be significant for the people in the long term.

Enclosed you will find a copy of the petition language and a statement regarding the goals of CEASE-FIRE Boston. We look forward to your swift and positive response.

Sincerely,

For the Committee
Jim Murray

the committee:

Andrew Schell   Patsy Donovan   Jim Murray   Boyce Slayman   Jose Vincenty
Mark Bourbeau   Richard McDonough   Tony Watson   Craig Lankhorst

James M. Murray

(Photo by Terri Davis. Boston, MA)

About The Author

James M. Murray is a concerned parent of a teenage son, a writer, teacher, and a long-time neighborhood activist. He was born and raised in Boston's inner-city, where he still resides.

In 1992, he organized **"CeaseFire, Boston"** (Citizens to Ensure A Safe Environment-Firearms Reduction Effort), a group of friends and neighbors were fed up with the shootings that plagued their community. He led a successful referendum advisory question on trying to ban handguns in their city. James is also cofounder of "Cease Fire, USA", in cooperation with his publisher, Robert D. Reed.

A contributing writer for the *Boston Globe*, James has written extensively on a variety of issues, specializing in elderly affairs. He teaches communications at Newbury College in Boston, where he is active in a number of community organizations. A graduate of Boston State College, he holds a master's degree in public affairs from the John W. McCormack Institute, University of Massachusetts at Boston. He is a U.S. Air Force veteran who served in Vietnam as a Security Policeman.

In 1993, James ran a grassroots campaign for Mayor of Boston (using his credit card and accepting no campaign contributions) to keep the issue of gun violence in the forefront of the mayoral debates. The *Boston Herald* called him, "...the true citizens' candidate." Although he was forced to end his campaign after a few months, the impact of his candidacy was felt. Eventually, the finalists in the election adopted his and the voters' position on handguns. In 1993, The Boston City Council approved a new law which prohibited the sale, transfer and possession of handguns to individuals under the age of 21. Sponsors of the legislation pointed to the results of the CeaseFire referendum as documented evidence of the desire of the people of Boston for such action.

(OK to photocopy this form.)

Share Your Ideas About Gun Violence! Reading *50 Things You Can Do About Guns* is only a beginning. Your ideas are important and should be shared with others. Please send us any of your ideas to help end gun violence. Write to us at the address below.

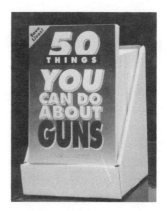

Order Books & Help Stop Gun Violence!

Use this book to help make your community safe. Each copy of *50 Things You Can Do About Guns* costs $9.95 (includes shipping, handling, and tax). Save on larger orders. Five copies cost $29.75; ten copies cost $40.00. You may purchase 12 books with a display unit for only $48.00 each. Resell the books for $96.00 and earn $48.00 for your organization. **Please help us to control costs by sending payment with all orders.**

Send _____ copies at a cost of $_____. Thank you.

Ship to:

Name:_____

Organization:_____

Address:_____

City:_____State:_____Zip:_____

Telephone:_____Fax:_____

Order books from the publisher:

Robert D. Reed
750 La Playa, Suite 647, San Francisco, CA 94121
Telephone: 1-800-PR-GREEN